Escapism

To order additional copies, please contact us.
BookSurge, LLC
www.booksurge.com
1-866-308-6235
orders@booksurge.com

Escapism

Jim Adduci

2006

Escapism

You can't hide,
it's all inside —

Jim Q.

CONTENTS

I dedicate these thoughts to the greatest man I ever knew; my Dad. A quiet, hardworking, family man; but when he spoke we all listened, because it was either the truth or it was funny. What else could you ask of a human being?

PREFACE

This is a compilation of my poems, essays, short stories, and thoughts while in prison. Do not let the word, *poems* scare you away. My poems are written for the everyday person, like me. These are not the poems you had to read in school, where you asked; "What the hell does that mean?" My poems are... intense. They come from the heart, along with a little blood, sweat and tears.

There are no earth-shaking revelations contained here-in. At least, I don't think so. You'll be the judge of that. All I know is that after I finished writing and put down my pen, I felt good. Even if I wrote something unpleasant or painful, it still made me feel good. As if I accomplished something important; and also the fact that it will last because it's down on paper. People can "talk a good talk," but so many times it's forgotten; "in one ear and out the other." My thoughts will be around for a long time because I took the time to write them down. So each item is like a snap-shot of my mind/feelings at that moment.

Like I said, there's nothing that will "blow you away," but I'm sure you'll be somewhat impressed. And after specific writings you will cry because you will see yourself, your family, and your friends; and you will remember your childhood. If you find yourself saying, "Wow," or "Cool," then that's enough for me. As you will see, I write simple and to the point. I don't have much of an education, but I've been around and know "stuff."

This is where I would like to thank my family for being the best bunch of people I've ever met; and for always loving me and supporting me, no matter what. And a special thanks to God for giving me my father; the nicest, smartest, most loving, hardest working, most caring human being I have ever known.

If it weren't for my family, I wouldn't be the man I am. In fact, if I could be just half the man my father was, I would be a lucky man; but I'm running out of time.

Why didn't I listen to his advice? I could have saved myself and everyone involved a lot of heartache. In the words of George Bernard Shaw, "Youth is wasted on the young." Or, Bob Dylan; "I was so much older then, I'm younger than that now."

Well back to the issue at hand. I hope you enjoy my writings and maybe even learn something that helps you in life's journey.

LOVE AND PEACE,
JIM

PS: Some of the writings will have a lead-in. It's not to explain the poems and stories. It's to explain where, why or when it was written.

INTRODUCTION

If there is a theme to this book, it is this: that there is no theme—no 'rhyme or reason'—just like you and me.

But, if you are looking for a meaning to your life (and not for "the meaning of life"), look at your accomplishments. What we actually accomplish says it all. Not what we want to accomplish or dream about doing, but what we succeed in doing. From large accomplishments to small, they all count; doing the work you enjoy, raising a happy family, walks on the beach or in the woods with your children, planting a garden, painting the house, volunteering some time to your community.

What we do with our lives is all up to us, just as what you do with this book and the information contained within is up to you. I originally wrote down my thoughts and daydreams just so my family could know and understand me a little better. But if you can get enjoyment and learn from my writings, then I will have accomplished something and that will mean a lot to me.

CHAPTER ONE

POEMS

This was written after about 6 months in prison. After I read the finished product I became very depressed, so I wrote the follow-up poem right away. I wrote it from a woman's point of view.

THE ESSENCE OF LIFE IS TIME

"HEY, BUDDY, GOT THE TIME?"

Dear God,

My Time is your Time,
Grant me more Time,
So I may love You for all Time,
I know this chance at life will be my last Time.

I had that special moment in Time,
During the years of my play Time,
That feeling of never running out of Time,
Which had me misusing this valuable Time.

The child plays in the morning Time,
The teenager plays at noon Time,
The adult plays at the night Time,
And the sun rises and sets, Time after Time.

Now that I find myself in my twilight Time,
My lord, my God, "The Keeper of Time",
Is there by any chance, some spare Time?
"Sorry my child, you're out of Time".

Oh no! You're wrong!
I'll look to the sky and raise my fist
And shout out loud, "You're wrong!"
Dare I?
Talk to the Lord, so firm and loud?
Maybe not wrong, just mistaken.

There must be time for me –
Because I breathe.
So if I live, I will survive,
Because of that special something
You put inside——instinct –
That inborn drive to stay alive.

If you knock me down, I'll get up again,
I'll fight for life, 'til the day I die.
As long as I take in the air you give,
That's a sign you want me to live.

As long as I live, I have the time
To mend the hearts I broke –
In doing so, I'll fix mine.
With my mind so clear,
I'll pack my bags and get out of here,
To the brand new world that was always there,
I was just too drunk and high to really care.

When I came in, I thought I died,
I said to myself, "This is the end."
I lost my man, my lover –
More importantly, I lost my friend.

I'm going home to start anew,

But if there's none, and neither you,
I'll work and pray and build me one.
I'll go to church and do good deeds,
A man I'll find by not looking for one.
I'll help the old and help the young,
My time I'll use for every one.

And all along he was there,
I just never noticed—like the sun.
His beauty is in his eyes,
His love is in his hands by what they do.

I'll use my time in the best possible way,
I'll love my life and I'll pray,
That my lord will say to me,
"Here my dear, this guy's for you."
This test of yours my Lord, was fine,
You had to be sure I learned the value of Time.

These gifts You gave me –
My life, my man, my baby –
I will thank you God,
'til the end of Time.

Again, from a woman's point of view.

A DAY TO CALL YOUR OWN

A noise brings you back from a velvety dream
Because someone waved his magic wand,
And brought the sun to you in streams
You must have heard the "crack of dawn."

You drag yourself from room to room
The same routine, the same fortune –
To water, clothes, lipstick and perfume,
You ask yourself, "Why do days start much too soon?"

Grab your keys and out the door
Down the street you pass the beach,
In the car a song hits your core
Which makes you think—you deserve much more.

Than to work and work and never play
Who made these rules up anyway?
One thing's for sure, to yourself you say –
It may not be much, but I deserve today!

Back home again you pack a bag
With things you need for a beach day,
What's left to do? But to call a friend –
Who wants to play.

And to your surprise
He says, "OK."
It seems you've found another –

That deserves "a day."
You've packed a bag with nuts and fruit
And cheese and crackers, and ice cold juice,
You've put on clothes that are cool and loose,
And underneath—a little bathing suit.

You sit on the porch and wait for him,
You hear the waves and smell the air,
It doesn't matter that the house cost an "arm and a limb,"
What's important, is the beach is near.

He arrives wearing shorts and a smile,
Takes you by the hand, and you walk that quarter mile –
To the place of sand,
That will be your home for a while.

You spread out your blanket
And set up your chairs,
You look around and see –
You're the first ones there.

He touches your face
And gives you a kiss,
And says, "Thanks for inviting me –
To such a place as this."

You lay on the blanket
And for the first time realize,
How tall he is –
And his green- hazel eyes.

You lay in the warmth of the morning sun
Watching the seagulls float in the sky,
This is your day—your day of fun,
The sand covers your toes, as you let out a sigh.

With the sun straight above,
It's time for a swim,
The water covers your body like a hand in a glove,
You ride the waves, and laugh with him.

The mothers and children have come to play,
With their radios and yelling, and the waves in the
      background.
But nothing can ruin this beautiful day –
'Cause you've turned all that noise into delightful "beach
      sounds."

You lay on the sand, in the hot summer heat,
As the baby oil is caressed, close to your "seat" –
Shoulder to shoulder, from your neck to your feet,
'Cause this is your day, and you deserve such a treat.

The day started with "peace and quite" –
Then "welcomed noise," that resembled a "riot."
The collection of shells and seaside "gems,"
And those sweet soft kisses, every now and then.

The time has come for the mothers to go home,
And the kids pack-up and leave you alone –
So you can talk and laugh, and drink champagne,
And walk hand and hand, down lover's lane.

Into a "flavor of colors" the "cherry sun" does sink —
It's a "Hendrix" color of yellow and gold; purple and pink.
The beach, the day, and your date has been great,
And now this sunset, is just "icing on the cake."
10/13/90

two people on the beach, flooded with moonlight:

man: "isn't this amazing? how bright it is at one o'clock at night! i mean so much moonlight gives this night such a special feel—an air of excitement!"

woman: "yes, it's beautiful."

they held hands and walked along the edge of other worlds. the damp sand and warm gentle breeze added to the excitement.
he ran ahead and did a cartwheel.
he ran into the shiny water and stamped his feet.
he skipped back to her side, let out a laugh and hugged her.

"you sure do enjoy yourself, don't you?"

"no, I don't enjoy myself, i enjoy everything else!"

"don't you think you're over doing it? i mean it's a nice night and the moon is out, but we have plenty of nights like this."

"no, no, we don't. we only have about three months of warm weather, and not every night is this warm. we only have a full moon once a month, and we don't always have time to enjoy it. time is precious; and so are moments such as these."

"as these?"

"yes, i can gaze at the moon and the stars; i can absorb the sparkling waves in the moonlight; i can smell the aroma of the sea mixed with the warm summer night; and when my eyes come back to you, i am dazzled all over again."

she smiled.

"and now the moon sparkles off your teeth as it shows me the beauty of your face."

she reached up and kissed him.

"thank you, that was sweet."

"because you're sweet, lovable, adorable, captivating, delightful…"

"stop, you're making me blush."

"but it's true. you are deserving of all these compliments; and compliments are 'earned', so don't shy away from them, accept them with pride and a sense of accomplishment"……. "i stop in mid-thought, and on bended knee, kiss the hand of a princess; and in the presence of a million stars and our one and only moon, i pledge my undying love to you—for all the women in the world are only stars, but you are my one and only moon."

he bent his head and kissed her soft, delicate hand.

upon rising, he picked up a piece of driftwood and slid it under his belt.

"what's the stick for?"

"this my darling is a sword and it is well known that the blood-thirsty dragon lives up ahead, somewhere. i must be prepared to defend my love with no regard of my own safety."

she giggled.

"it's so much fun spending time with you."

"thank you my lady, and i accept the compliment with 'pride and accomplishment.' princess, if i may be serious for a moment."

"yes?"

"you see, i fool around because if i didn't, the world would crush my spirit. the injustices and the suffering of the innocent are everywhere. i know some day all will be set right, but the time table is much too slow for my liking, so in the meantime—i play. abraham lincoln said, 'people are about as happy as they set their mind to be' (or something to that affect) 'if you keep the child inside, you'll never grow old', i said that."

he took her hand.

"come walk with me and smell the nighttime roses that only grow by moonlight."

"where?"

"they're everywhere, if you believe."

they walked, they looked, they listened. she collected 'moon-shells'- the ones that sparkled in the night light.

he slayed a dragon.

the moon inched across the sky as they talked about their dreams and hidden secrets. they returned safely to his summer cottage—an old, weather-beaten, run down, shack of a place. standing there, looking at it in the moonlight, it looked haunted. she wondered what did the most damage, the winter storms or the summer parties?

he scooped her up into his arms, climbed the rickety stairs and kicked open the door.

"welcome to my castle."

they went inside.

ONE IN THE SAME

The sun is the most important thing in my life, for it makes my existence possible by giving nourishment to the "foods" which in turn nourish me.

It brings pleasure to my eyes by lighting up the beauty of "mother earth" with its forests and mountains, from which crystal clear water flows down through the countryside to the rivers, lakes and seas.

And in much the same way, as the reward of heaven at the end of our life, is the reward of a sunset at the end of our day. A glorious, magnificent, wonderful sunset! And it's not just something I can see, I can feel it when its warmth touches me.

The sun makes me laugh when I swim and play. And when it sets behind the clouds, leaving a mix of shades of colors, it overwhelms me. I sit and bask in the sun and it nourishes my soul. It makes me glad I'm alive.

Now let's see.....

It's the most important thing in my life.

It brings pleasure to my eyes.

It's my reward at the end of the day.

When it touches me, I can feel its warmth.

It makes me laugh.

And at times it overwhelms me.

It nourishes my soul.

It makes me glad that I'm alive.

Gee, what do you know,

My son does the same thing!

THE CRYBABY

It's something I can't help,
I started life this way
With a scream and a yelp.
It's not my fault,
It was just a cry for help!

And until I hit the age of reason,
I would cry so many times
All through the many seasons.
But of course my mother would say,
For many a good reason!

From boyhood to manhood,
I would cry a few more times
From falls and breaks brought on from brotherhood.
But the most painful hurt of all,
Was caused by the sweet nourishment of womanhood!

God's golden light brings sounds and sights –
Roosters crow and dogs "chitchat",
Flowers open and birds to flight.
All God's beauty creates a tear in my eye,
Sunsets, birds to nest, flowers close—'tis night!

Streams, rivers, oceans and seas –
From love and touch, babies come
To sticks and balls and autumn leaves.
Grown and gone, toys with spider webs,
These things and more bring tears to me!

And so I started as a crybaby,
Most lessons in life came hard,
But were made easy by those who loved me.
Sky, flowers and lost toys bring tears,
And so I'll gladly finish as –
A big crybaby!

EVERLASTING LOVE

The toys of morning fade
As the toys of day appear,
But nighttime brings them all back home
Because of how we care.

Those special toys, those caring toys,
Those daily toys and worn out toys.
The ones that listened while we cried –
Trying to explain "why."

At times my teddy bear was missing
And the world was not right,
The family would not stop looking
Until I held it oh so tight.

And the teddy bear said,
"What was he thinking?
What was in his head?
He abandoned me –
Left me for dead!"

Oh no, oh no, I just went away
To do the things we must –
To live through the day.

And all the while, inside I knew
We'd meet again at night,
I'd talk to you
And tell you what was new.

Dear darling toy, oh precious toy
I could never ever leave you!
The timeless hours we spent together
Mean you're part of me and I'm part of you.

SHADOWS

'Children of the Sun'

At sunrise they appear, so light and faint,
As if to say -
They're not sure, if they should be here.
But as the sun grows tall,
The shadows grow dark, as if to say —
Yes, we have a right to be here.
For right they are,
Where ever we go——they are.
As a guardian angel is sent from heaven,
Shadows are sent from just as far.

All through our lives, from start to end,
They're at our side, through thick and thin.
They run, they jump with us,
And in the game of "copy-cat" —
There's no doubt who would win.
They're short, they're fat, tall or round,
They're mostly found flat on the ground.
They can stand up straight and walk a wall,
And at the corner have a harmless fall.

Where do they go on rainy days?
Just like us, they need a holiday.
And when we're sick, with a heavy head,
They lie beside us in our bed.

The plane, from whence it comes
Travels high in the sky,
But the shadow skims across the ground
Because it is afraid to fly.

They're in our songs, and in our shows —
"The Shadow of your Smile," and "Me and My Shadow."
And of course, "The Shadow Knows" —
From old time radio.

The Indians respected someone's shadow
For fear it could be part of his soul,
The same with trees and buildings, plants and rocks
All inanimate objects—so I'm told.

You're all alone, late at night
The candles you light, bring you shadows of fright,
From the corner of your eye
You catch those dark little things —
That go scurrying by.
You light some more
And place your chair beside the wall,
You check the windows and lock the door.

If your loved one is gone
And all night you sit alone,
Light a candle just before dawn
And you'll find you're not alone.

You sit at the table and talk to the wall,
The image you're seeing is dark and tall.
Memories float by —
Of a strawberry kiss and a loving caress —

Which brings tears to your eyes.
You lean over to touch it,
In your heart there's no doubt.
And ever so gently you kiss the "dark" –
"It" disappears, and the candle goes out.

Shadows are part of us, each and every one,
And they will always be –
'Cause they are, *children of the sun.*

Stephen is a close friend of mine who got hit by a car late at night while crossing the street. He was close to death with brain damage, but pulled through. He cannot speak and has trouble walking.

TO ALL THE STEPHENS

Good morning world,
I breathe still.
Of sights and sounds
I'll get my fill.
To see the light, to hear the word
I don't have to go up the hill –
For earth abounds, all around,
From sky to ground it can be found.
And in our mind it all resides
For us to enjoy at our will.

Life gets hard, then harder still.
The emptiness you feel is good –
Because it's real.
It's part of life to be depressed,
So let your mind relax and take a rest.
Then, when you try, you'll do your best.

When morning comes you'll see the light,
And you'll say, "Sun."
With children running about,
You'll hear their sounds,
And you'll say, "Fun."

Life goes on,
What's done is done.
All you need is what you have –
The love of family,

Your determination to grow,
The love of Jesus —

Who owns your soul.
So in the morning, say hello to Him.
Offer the day's joys and troubles up to Him.
And what comes back, is a gift from Him.

So make the best of what you have,
'Cause there's people in the world with less than you.
All you can do is try and pray.
And just remember Christ's gift to you —
Besides His love
Is "each and every day."

Terry
The Beginning is The End

There once was a little girl.
And oh, how they loved her,
For she was their very first baby -
that special bond that made them a family.
On Sundays they would dress her up
And talk to her, play with her and walk with her.
So proudly they would show her off -
For this is just the first—there's more to follow.
And as their angel slept, they would sit
By her side and dream of her future.
But in all their dreams only one stood out -
That she would be safe and happy.
And in all their dreams, they never dreamt,
That their baby would have 7 babies of her own.
And when she did, they hinted that she should slow
    down,
For if she didn't, she may go broke -
When Santa came to town!
So time moved on, and all her babies grew,
From cocoon, to caterpillar, to butterflies;
All so beautiful, good, and true.
Like everyone must, they went through hard times.
But all through the years, they shared their laughs and
    tears
For that's the "stuff" that bonds family -
When people share and care.
Together now, they all look back and view the past

through adult eyes -
The hardships she endured they now realize.
And oh, how they love her,
For how she has survived, and managed to keep -
That little girl inside.

"TO THOSE WHO KNOW"

a sniffle and a swallow
brings back the "the taste" of old tomorrows.
it stops me in my tracks,
I find a chair and, in contemplation sit back.
could it be? was it possible?
that the tiniest amount
could hide out for 15 months,
and wait its turn, and find its time –
to become my, "one last line?"
I close my eyes and swallow again,
only to find, that the taste remained.
which means only one thing –
that cocaine is heading to my brain!
and all those thoughts, stored in my memory,
come rushing back—to attack?
for cocaine is my enemy, or so I'm told,
but all my memories are interesting, exciting and bold.
except the "morning after", when responsibility called,
and of course the two times I almost died –
but who counts the "close calls?"
for if we paid attention, we'd have no fun;
and nothing would get done.
we wouldn't climb the highest trees,
nor drive the fastest cars, nor build the tallest buildings.
we wouldn't fly the highest jets,
and of course—go to the moon.
"excitement" is progress; it's a learning experience
it's one reason we take our "highs" -
and "chase the dragon."

but some of these things can be done
sitting in our living room.
the "Moody Blues" once told us
that "thinking is the best way to travel";
but they neglected to tell us, that some people's brain –
just seems to unravel!
the trick is not to abuse it,
we are supposed to hold it all together –
every time we "use" it.
many memories are made up of words –
they're the "magic" of conversation,
they're a verbal sensation -
to get our point of view across.
but it's true, at the "meeting of the minds,"
during the act of communicating,
the thought could be lost
because out of the blue –
you wish you were fornicating!
"Enough already with the talk," your mind is telling you.
you've taken care of your intellect,
now it's time to take care of . . .
you look at your clock.
if you could only stop time, at your choosing,
then you'd never cry, over what you're loosen –
for all good things come to an end.
even, sadly, the love of a friend.
the "eyes of love" tell our heart
what it wants to feel and see,
so the truth is real -
only to you; or me.
but once the eyes and heart are opened to reality,
the heart breaks

and tears flow free.
bad as it seems
it's not that bad,
in fact, with time
comes the sweet memories.
and the mind goes on –
like a vacuum, the more you think,
the more it sucks thoughts from out of "nowhere."
so, I sit and stare out the window
at the flowers, trees and birds flying by –
I wonder, just how long have the birds gone by;
and how long will they continue to do so?
or will the nuclear problem "explode,"
making everything lifeless and cold?
will this nuclear thing of the 40's –
this answer to our energy problem –
in reality be our downfall,
or will it be the common cold?
so I close my eyes and start a dream
that I will never finish,
for there's always someone
that comes or calls
who, at that time, is needed –
as much as a teenager needs a blemish.
so I'll file this dream with the million others –
the dreams of adventure, filled with courage,
the dreams of fancy, flight and song;
and the sexy ones that happen under the covers
with the universal woman –
with dark eyes and hair so long.
I heard this once before
so I'll say it again for you

'cause it's all been said before
(there's nothing that's really new),
we all must have our dreams
no matter how unlikely,
the reason being –
"only a dreamer can have a dream come true."
I opened my eyes to meet my "interruption,"
and to get on with my life –
the trials and tribulations; the toil and strife.
but to my surprise and much to my delight,
stood my "universal woman"
who, I'm sure, would stay with me
all through-out the night.
whether real or fake, this is a dream
that will make a lasting memory.
and as far as my original question –
"could this be my one last line?"
it couldn't be,
it would have made me talk,
and all I had –
was a "simple" thought.

~

My first love
AS TIME GOES BY

A lovely breeze did come my way
And cooled me from the troubled day,
But oh too soon it went away -
I pray it comes another day.

The earth in me says DAMN!
I have lost another "thing"- a most precious thing.
The spirit in me says, whatever thou will, God
You can aim, direct and then change again, my life.

And reasons pass me by—until time does,
And I say, ah, I see why.
But in the mean time, my being aches -
As from a baby the sweets you take
So as it should—it cries,
Until time goes by.

At her I cannot yell,
There's nobody I can really tell
Of the good and bad in life's wishing well,
I guess that's why there's heaven and hell.

TIME / LOVE

It's everywhere, but can't be held,
Without it there's no life.
We need it each and every day,
It's day and night, it's warm and bright.

6/6/90

A friend brought a girl to me 6 months before my release, so I could start "relating" with girls again. Wendi was just what the doctor ordered——hot, sexy, open-minded and very giving. I could touch, kiss and hold her. If it were the 60's, she would be a flower child.

TIMELESS DREAMS

My heart was given, my soul was taken
There were no yesterdays, only tomorrows.
It was all so unexpected, she touched me with her lips
I lost my heart, because I left it unprotected.
My dreams soared over the wall
And found rainbows and waterfalls,
Sunsets, stars and satin sheets;
And there were caresses and kisses
From her head to her feet,
But only in my mind 'cause my body's confined.
She took my soul and ran away
So I wait and wait, and wait for days.
We can live without money, power or friends,
But a soul is our "essence" until the very end.
So I close my eyes perchance to dream,
To mend my mind, and hide from time.

2/8/92

SHARING / CARING

People come and go
with a "How do you do?"
or just a friendly, "Hello."
They smile and talk before they say,
"Oh my, it's late! I'm sorry,
but I really must go."
And in most cases it's not what's said,
it's the time that's spent -
That really matters.
So I'll thank you for your time
And these things you gave me
Which are now mine -
The blanket that keeps my bod so warm and cozy,
The moisturizer that covers my bod from head to toesy,
The food that makes my bod big and strong,
The visits that make my soul sing a song -
"yippy eye, yippy aye,
Oh Happy Day!"

10/19/91

for all the hungry people
for all the times we stepped over the homeless
for all the lonely people
for all the people laying in hospital beds
for all the people at home whose bed is their prison
for all the households filled with violence, instead of love
for all the times a father had to return home without a job
for all the times a wife has been beaten
for all the times a child has been cruelly punished
for all the times that insults and rocks have been tossed at
　　　　a child who's different
for all the times that teenagers and parents yelled at each
　　　　other rather than listening
for all the times a mother's tears have fallen in vain
for all the times young hearts were broken in their first
　　　　lesson in love
for all the times seasoned hearts were broken as they
　　　　watched their lover turn and walk away
for all the times tears rolled down someone's face as they
　　　　took another hit or did just one more line
for all the people that are lost and don't know it
for every day that went by that friends, lovers, sisters and
　　　　brothers did not speak to each other out of anger
for all the people who tried and failed...

I cry
but that's not enough,
I must try...

to share my food, money and time
to stop and talk
to share my knowledge and give advice

to play with the children, and in that way teach
to comfort them in their loneliness and confusion
to offer support and direction for the abused women,
    children and animals
to help mend love's broken hearts
to show the drug user a better way
to tear down the wall of non-communication
to replace anger with patience and understanding
to give a pat on the back to those who failed and say,
    "Hey, at least you tried."

But it would be all so much easier with your help.

3/8/92

A THANKSGIVING DAY POEM?

From England came the Puritans,
Then the Franklin's, the Washington's and Jefferson's.
From France came the money
To finance our fight for Independence.

From Italy came the Mafia -
The Capone's, the Anguilo's and Patriaca's,
And mixed in with the "Big Guys"
Were the pizza makers, cobblers and "Families of
    Produce"

Organized crime became disorganized
And all the bosses went to jail.
The cobblers have all but disappeared,
And the pizzas have become "Americanized."

And even though the supermarkets have crushed the
corner grocer,
There emerges one family (as the Phoenix from the
    ashes).
And through love, devotion and determination,
Will not fail to build a family dynasty,
That will rival the DuPonts, the Rockefellers and the
    mighty Kennedy's!
(as soon as Jim gets out of jail)

11/18/90

IT'S DONE WITH MIRRORS

When I get what I want in my struggle for wealth
And the world makes me king for a day,
Just go to the mirror and look at myself
And see what that person has to say.

For it isn't my father or mother or wife
Upon whose judgment I pass,
The fellow whose verdict counts most in my life
is the one staring back from the glass.

Some people may think I'm a straight-shooting chum
and call me a wonderful guy,
But the one in the glass says you're only a bum
If you can't look him straight in the eye.

He's the fellow to please, never mind with all the rest
For he's with you clear to the end,
And you've passed your most dangerous, difficult test
If the man in the glass is your friend.

I may fool the whole world down the pathway of years
and get pats on the back as I pass,
But my final reward will be heartaches and tears
If I've cheated the man in the glass.

Anonymous

IF...

If you think you are beaten, you are.
If you think you dare not, you don't.
If you like to win, but you think you can't
It is almost certain you won't.

If you think you'll lose, you're lost,
For out of the world we find,
Success begins with a fellow's will—
It's all in the state of mind.

If you think you are outclassed, you are,
You've got to think high to rise,
You've got to be sure of yourself before
You can ever win a prize.

Life's battles don't always go
To the stronger or faster man,
But sooner or later the man who wins
Is the man who Thinks He Can!!!

Anonymous

CHAPTER TWO

ESSAYS

and

SHORT STORIES

A true story

The Butterfly
or
Unspoken Love

It's Saturday, about 1:00 PM in the month of August, and it's hot. But lucky me, I'm on the beach, walking the edge of the water. It's the kind of beach that's just right for walking—with flat wet sand that stretches for about three miles, no rocks and occasionally a large sea clam (shut tight, waiting to be thrown back into the ocean), and a few empty sea shells. The water is comfortably cool and crystal clear.

The beach is almost full, but it's large, so there's enough room for everyone. I'm walking with a friend and we're talking politics, the economy and "how and when" we're going to get rich. Oh ya, and checking out the babes (probably the oldest "spectator sport" there is, and understandably so).

That's why I was a bit surprised that I noticed the butterfly lying in the wet sand. With my friend and I deep in conversation, and our heads going back and forth (trying to catch all the "feminine" sights) my eyes still focused on the butterfly about ten feet in front of us. It was a habit I held on to from my childhood—scanning the ground for change or other "valuable" things.

I bent down to get a look at its beautifully designed wings, and I saw that it was still alive. That was another surprise because there were kids running in and out of the water, adults walking the edge in both directions, and yet no one had stepped on it.

Now comes the dilemma—what to do? It's soaking wet, and we're told not to touch a butterfly's wings or they won't be able to fly. The easy thing to do (and it would have been the accepted response) would be to shake my head and say, "What a shame," and continue walking. But I can't just leave it there in the wet sand, helpless and with death inevitable. So I "dig" under it with my hands, and lift up slowly. The water is drained out of the sand, which puts the butterfly on semi-dry sand in the palm of my hand. Little by little I let the sand fall from my hand until only the butterfly remains. I'm now holding one wet, sandy butterfly in my right hand. What to do?

We continue walking as I hold the butterfly flat in my hand. Slowly the sun dries out the wings, and every now and then I gently blow on them, which blows away the grains of sand that have dried out. This goes on for an hour or so. By the time our walk is completed and we're back where we started, the butterfly is "flexing" its wings. I hold out my hand, and the butterfly flutters away into the warm day, and disappears with a gentle breeze. I feel good. If it weren't for me, surely the wet sand would have been its grave. In the eyes of the world, an insignificant accomplishment; in the eyes of Jesus, a kindly act. I felt good.

Patience, kindness, compassion and intelligence saved that butterfly. Apply these same virtues to the "children" and the reward will be the same; as when I held out my hand, showed the world to the butterfly and watched it dance away into the day—into the future. We only can do our best; the rest is up to God.

4/10/91

LIMITED HOURS

Butterfly of love
Land on my shoulder,
Butterfly of love
Say it's not over.

Bring to me
The message from God,
That my time has come
To be happy and free.

Let me flex my wings
And feel the warm sun,
Free me from the quicksand,
Let my suffering be done.

We have many seasons
Here on Earth,
But to lose just one
There is no good reason.

I must go to the flowers,
There is not time to waste
For I, like the butterfly,
Have limited hours.

This passage touches on one's childhood and being in
    prison; but most importantly, that life takes on a new
    meaning when viewed through the heart.

"Till the heart be touched"

Here I sit in my old accustomed chamber, where I used to sit in days gone by...Here I have written many tales, many that have been burned to ashes, many that have doubtless deserved the same fate. This claims to be called a haunted chamber, for thousands upon thousands of visions have appeared to me in it; and some few of them have become visible to the world. If ever I should have a biographer, he ought to make great mention of this chamber in my memoirs, because so much of my lonely youth was wasted here, and here my mind and character were formed; and here I have been glad and hopeful, and here I have been despondent. And here I sat a long, long time waiting patiently for the world to know me, and sometimes wondering why it did not know me sooner, or whether it would ever know me at all—at least till I were in my grave. And sometimes it seems to me if I were already in the grave, with only life enough to be chilled and benumbed. But oftener I was happy—at least as happy as I then knew how to be, or was aware of the possibility of being. By and by the world found me out in my lonely chamber, and called me forth—not, indeed, with a loud roar of acclamation, but rather with a still small voice—and forth I went, but found nothing in the world I thought preferable to my solitude till now...And now begin to understand why I was imprisoned so many years in this lonely chamber and why I could never break through the viewless bolts and bars; for if I had sooner made my escape into the world, I should have grown hard and rough, and been covered with earthly dust, and my heart might have become callous by rude encounters with the multitude...But living in solitude till the fullness of time was come, I still kept the dew of my youth and the freshness of my heart...I used to think that I could imagine all passions, all feelings, and states of the heart and mind; but how little did I know?...Indeed, we are but shadows: we are not endowed with real life, and all that seems most real about us is but the thinnest substance of a dream—till the heart be touched. That touch creates us—then we begin to be—thereby we are beings of reality and inheritors of eternity.

Nathaniel Hawthorne
1840

When I was an inmate at Baystate Correctional Institution, we were allowed to walk an oval shaped dirt walkway in the back of the prison, until the fence went up.

"THE GRASS IS GREENER"

Today, October 18, 1990, "they" completed the fence. I have been transferred, without being moved, to another prison. For all practical purposes Baystate is now a medium prison.

I just walked the inside perimeter of the fence. I looked through the wire mesh at the dirt path I used to walk, and the grassy spots where I used to sit among the flowers.

The fence is up, there'll be:
no walks down the dirt path
no stopping to pick up strange looking rocks
no more picking up furry caterpillars and placing them in the grass, out of harm's way
no more picking leaves off the basil plants that I discovered, and bringing them to my room to dry out
no more walking into the field to get a closer look at the flowers, and the bees that visit them
no more walks on the tar road with cars driving by, leaving the "taste of freedom" in their wind

no more walking under the two water towers and sitting in their shade

no more sitting on the wall and watching the muskrats swim and disappear into one of the many holes in the side of the hill

no more sitting in "my" old, broken lawn chair (where I did some of my best thinking) to soak up the sun

no more unobstructed views of the hills, trees and sunset.

The horizon must now be observed around the corners of buildings, and through a fence that says, "Look, but don't touch." Without the fence, there always was the "possibility" that you could keep on walking and touch whatever you wanted. Possibility is just another word for "FREEDOM"

There is no joy in "Mudville" -
The fence is up.

Nature's Show

There's a night light on the outside of my building, right above my window, which has brought me hours of enjoyment. In the summer months I get to watch all types of bugs fly about the light. It's one of those new types of electric lights that has a golden tint to it, and has a beam that shines down on a certain area of land. The bugs will come out of total darkness into the beam of light, as if they appeared out of nowhere.

I remember it was the night of July 4th, and I was lying on my bed in a dark room and looking out the window at a variety of bugs. There were a bunch of new ones that flew in such a pattern that gave an impression of the old-fashion punks (sticks of compressed sawdust). They went "round-n-round" and in an erratic line of flight. When I was young I used to light these punks, blow out the flame and in the dark, make designs in the air with the glowing end. These bugs were now my punks.

Then there were the moths, all sizes and shapes. This one night a large moth was flying around the light, and because it was tan and under the golden beam of the light, it gave off a golden hue. Through the double pane window it gave a double image as if it had a gold aura. When it moved it left a trail of "gold dust," it was the closest thing to a real, live "Tinkerbelle."

In the spring and the fall my mind gets to play with the raindrops in the light beam and on the window.

The winter brings the snowflakes. Now, snowflakes

by themselves, observed closely from hand to eye, are extraordinarily unique. But with the opportunity to be able to watch them in flight, by way of an outside light which cast a golden hue; they become gold dust and at times golden nuggets with the dark, night time sky as the background. And you are bedazzled.

I lie in bed for hours watching this amazing, fantastic, incredible, spectacular show which nature has provided; the wind blowing the golden flakes downward at different speeds. Then, ceasing, allowing them to float, which permits a better look. Then an upward draft lifts them back up to the window, and chases them in every direction, until a downward draft pushes or pulls them into a collision course with earth. Thousands of snowflakes go "crashing" down to a "soft" landing onto their brothers and sisters.

In my wonderment, I am humbled.

7/7/91

"One night in the beginning of winter before the pond froze over, about nine o'clock, I was startled by the loud honking of geese, and stepping to the door, I heard the sound of their wings like a tempest in the woods as they flew low over my house."

Henry Thoreau, "Walden Pond"

Jim Adduci, "Baystate"

"I left the woods for as good a reason as I went there. Perhaps it seemed to me that I had several more lives to live, and could not spare any more time for that one."

Henry Thoreau

I must get on with my third life, the years of forty-to-sixty. There's so much to do, with plenty of time to spare, if only I start it soon.

Jim Adduci

11/25/90

OUR THREE GREATEST GIFTS

1)   FREE WILL –

It puts us in control of our life, future and destiny. It also gives us the responsibility to succeed or not to succeed; to love or to be alone; to laugh or to cry; "to be or not to be." It takes away the luxury of being able to blame others for our failures and our faults.

Animals live by instinct. Humans live by daily decisions, some more difficult than others and some seem to carry the weight of the world which, handled in the proper way, is what we have to gain—"the world."

Thank you God for this power, may I use it and not abuse it.

2)   THE EARTH –

In all its beauty, grandeur and "simple complexity" it sustains us with its food, water and air. It has become a living organism in its own right, and provides nourishment for us throughout our life. But through the misuse of our free will we have injured the earth by way of man-made pollution. It is "limping" to its death, and it is taking us with it, and rightly so.

Thank you God for this earth, may we use it and not abuse it.

3)   WOMAN –

In all her beauty, vitality, mystery and "simple complexity" she is our anchor, our home, and our hope. She replenishes mankind. She is our "Mother Earth." But alas, we abuse her by way of machoism and mindless hate, which accumulates into rape. Yes, we rape women; we rape the earth; and we rape ourselves by taking for granted these three gifts.

The sun has risen and a new day is born. May we, through our free will, decide to use, and not abuse, these gifts.

Thank you God for this second chance.

12/21/91

Jim

EARTH, WIND, FIRE AND WATER

EARTH-
This piece of space we call Earth,
is just a place of dirt and birth.
When united with wind, fire and water,
becomes our home—becomes our mother.

WIND-
Through the mountains and the valleys -
the wind talks,
But the answers to all our questions
are "Blown in the Wind,"
says the boy from Woodstock.

FIRE-
The day dawns to where we are,
The fire grows all day long,
Then becomes a morning star,
says the man from Walden Pond.

WATER-
Rain brings contemplation,
Rain brings growth,
Rain brings cleansing,
Rain brings hope.

8/2/91

BIRDS AND FISH

The birds look down into the water at the fish and think, *what a sad way to live—spending their whole life in the water and only being able to swim.*

The fish look up at the birds and think, *poor birds, not knowing the joy of swimming and being at the mercy of the weather—the heat and cold, the wind and rain.*

But what about flying fish? Yes there is a certain fish that can jump out of the water, spread its wing-type fins and "fly" about twenty feet!

Then there are certain ducks (loons) that dive to the bottom of the lake and "swim" along the bottom for food.

Was it their desire to fly or to swim? Or was it because no one told them they couldn't do it?

A POSSESSIVE LOVE IS NOT A TRUE LOVE;
IT IS A SELF-CENTERED, EGOTISTICAL LOVE.
TRUE LOVE DOES NOT TAKE;
IT GIVES.

FOOD CHAIN / LOVE CHAIN

I'm sitting at a picnic table writing, when I notice a flying ant in front of me. His wings seem to be stuck together and he's trying to free them, which seems to be a natural process. I watch him for a few minutes and see that the job is almost complete. I finish writing my sentence and when I look back, a spider has "my" ant in his mouth. I try to free it with a pen, but the spider fights me. He drops the ant in order to give full attention to the pen. I then notice that the ant is dead, so I pull the pen away and let the spider take him away.

I felt sorry for the ant because in those few short minutes, I grew attached. By hoping it would fix its wings and fly away, I had an interest in it. If the spider got a hold of some other ant, it wouldn't bother me—for he is just doing what is natural—but why my ant?

Why was it "my" ant? Because I gave it attention. I was hoping it would free its wings and fly away—that would make me smile—but that spider robbed me of that. So, was I more upset with the death of the ant, or with the fact that I lost a chance to smile?

At first you say, "Oh no!" concerning the ant. But, I'm not sure, think about it. You know spiders eat ants every day and it doesn't bother you. And on the other hand why not be happy for the spider for finding food?

Once again, because that was "my" ant.

Now, we move on to pets. We all know how much we love our pets—dogs, cats, hamsters, rabbits, birds, fish, snakes and lizards, and how attached become to them. We do as much as possible for our pets by giving them the right food, toys, blankets and pillows and attention. Even if we're busy and our dog or cat wants to be patted or scratched, we'll stop what we're doing and oblige them, because that's what we would like if we were in their shoes.

Our pets are an extension of ourselves. There is a little bit of us in them because of the love and attention we give them. I myself own a dog, or he owns me. I say that because in a sense he picked me to live with, in much the same way as a person goes to the pet store to pick out his pet. When my dog was a puppy he lived two streets away. He was brought to my house for a visit. He must have liked what he saw, because he ran away from his house and showed up on my door steps, time after time. So with the permission of the owner, I took him in. That was eleven years ago, and in that time we've been through "heaven and hell" together.

When I come home and he's jumping up and down, and barking with his tail wagging, I'm happy. When we're swimming, side by side and riding the waves, I can feel the excitement he's feeling. And when he's sick, I'm sad, depressed and "down in the dumps." I look forward to when he will be better, so I will be happy. He is a piece of me. Of course, I love all dogs, but he's special—just like that ant was special for those few minutes.

Now we move on to the most special kind of love—children—and even more special—your children.

Talk about something being an extension of you—a child is the ultimate. And as time goes on, you make it even more so by doing everything for them. You decide, for the most part, what food they'll eat, what clothes they'll wear, what school they'll attend. You give them some of your knowledge, through advice, but when they make mistakes and you have to punish them, you suffer along with them. They are a part of you, and all your love and dreams rest with them.

Now we move to the end of the "love chain," and find ourselves face to face with Jesus. When we're happy—He's happy, when we're sad—He's sad. His love and attention is constantly there for the taking.

Concerning the Ant and the Spider:

That was nature taking its course. Things die to make room for others. Maybe the spider hadn't eaten for days, and it was his time to live. The fact that it was my ant didn't matter, remember, I made it "my" ant. I put my hopes and desires into it; I set myself up for the fall. To the world it was just an ant, but to Jesus, and me, and the spider—it was special.

Concerning Our Pets:

We are all Jesus' pets. I mean that in a loving and caring way, not in an authoritative way, or as playthings. And he doesn't try to control us, as we do our pets. He gives us free will, so when we do screw-up, there is no one to blame but ourselves.

When we sin, Jesus is sad—in much the same way that we're sad when our pet is sick. And He can't wait for our soul to get better so He can smile once again.

Concerning the Child:

I mentioned how the child is the extension of ourselves, and so are we of God, because we are made in his image and likeness. He came to Earth to suffer and die for us, which gives Him a stake in our well-being, just as we have a stake in our children's well-being.

He gives us His time, His attention, and His love; as we give the ant, our pet, and our child.

Concerning Jesus:

You noticed when I discussed the ant, the pet, and the child, I talked about Jesus—it can't be helped. Jesus is "involved" with us, whether we know it or not.

All He wants for us is what we want—to be healthy, happy and good. To be good, we just follow Jesus' advice, so when our time comes, we will be united with Him, and the "love chain" will be complete.

This was written with some exaggeration and humor.
My sister means the world to me.

"The Lamp"

This is a story of how a simple, everyday, inanimate object, such as a lamp, can cause a healthy, mentally well-balanced, "two-feet-on-the-ground" type of guy to confuse his reality with fantasies; to fall into depression which leads to an act of violence, then finally to "madness". It's a sad story. And let me, at this time; warn you all—it can happen to you if you have a sister. The type of sister who, on the outside is caring, loving, helpful and sweet; but on the inside is a conniving, diabolical, heartless woman, who can hold a grudge for 30 years or so, concerning an arm being ripped-off her favorite doll in the heat of play-time. It's the only reason I can come up with. I know you're saying that's a minor offense, and you're probably right. It must be the confused state of mind I've been in. Things just haven't been the same since the lamp came into my life.

Let me start at the beginning. A while back I got myself into a mess of trouble concerning drugs and ended up in prison. I realized my mistakes and decided to put things in the past and try to make the most of my time by reading and writing. I really enjoyed writing. I wrote stories, poems, letters, and essays—anything that took me away from the reality of being in prison.

The problem with the lamp started when my cellmate finished his sentence and went home, taking his lamp with him. I had an overhead light, so I could still write, but it wasn't the same. I needed a desk lamp. It gave me a cozy feeling; sitting in a small, dark room, absorbed in my writing at my little desk. The fact that it was a little desk plays an important role in this story, as you will see.

During one of my visits, I casually mentioned that I missed having a desk lamp. My sister, for the sake of privacy, we'll call "Terry," instantly volunteered to get one for me. If only I realized then of her devious plan, this story of "the lamp" wouldn't be necessary. I say necessary because I hope to save others who are in similar situations—no not in prison—I mean with a sister who is cheerfully offering to do something for you. Stop and think—could this be the start of her "master plan" for revenge?

I had a hint of "something in the making" during the months of visits from Terri and my mother, who for reasons of privacy we'll call "Mom." So many times they would say that they would bring me Chinese food "sometime," or that they went to the restaurant but it was closed, or that maybe the next time they would bring some. I would go back to my cell with a craving for Chinese food, and have to settle for dry crackers with peanut butter and wash it down with water.

Well, Sunday came again and so did they—with a cold cut sandwich for me. They mumbled something about a Chinese holiday and the place being closed, but it didn't bother me because I learned not to pay attention to them during my visits. I would just eat whatever they brought, as Mom would pick on Terri about her driving, and Terri would come back with a quick, witty reply like, "Oh, yea!" I was almost through with my slice of banana bread, which my mother made with peanuts, raisins, vegetable oil (instead of butter) and chunks of cheese (because she wanted to try something new) when Terri said, in a strange tone now that I think of it, "I have a desk lamp for you."

The visit went as usual with my mother getting three cups of tea out of the same tea bag, and Terri eating the seafood salad that my mother brought for me. But that didn't matter; all that did matter was that I was getting a desk lamp! Now I would be able to write my novel.

My lamp had to stay in the property room overnight, to be placed on my property list before I could get it. I said a prayer that nothing would happen to it. They called me down to pick it up about 10:00 the next morning. I was walking with a bounce and singing, "I'm going to get my lamp, I'm going to get my lamp." When I saw the box it was in, I stopped in my tracks. Gee, it looks awfully big I thought, but I signed for it and took it back to my room. In the room it felt like Christmas—tearing the paper off it and folding back the cardboard flaps, to get my first look at my lamp.

"Oh my God!" I said. I had asked for a small lamp with a wood base and a beige colored lampshade, less than a foot high, so it would fit nicely on my desk. What I got was a lamp about a foot and a half high with a brass base and a large, green, glass dome.

The sayings "Don't look a gift horse in the mouth," and "A bird in the hand is worth two in the bush," came to me. At least I had a lamp. I took it out of the box, placed it on the desk and plugged it in. I put my hand on it to center it on the desk, and the light came on very dim. I removed my hand for a second, and then picked it up looking for the light switch, and the light got brighter. I placed it back on the desk and touched it again and it got brighter—again, and the light went out.

I pulled the chair up to the table and sat in front of the lamp—there was no switch. Slowly I reached over and touched the lamp with my fingertips—the light went on. I touched it again—it got brighter, again—brighter, again—it went out. Wow! Not only did I have the most unique lamp in the prison, but I had something that would give me hours of "entertainment." Little did I know what was in store for me.

The aggravation started that night. At first it didn't bother me, but I noticed by the end of the night that I was in a pissed-off mood. The problem was, when I would move my pad of paper, or reach for my tea or my pen, I would accidentally touch the base of the lamp and the light would go out. I would then have to touch it three times, in order to put it back to bright. The first touch was very dim, the second touch was okay, but the third one was just right. I would be in the middle of a thought, writing like crazy, and I would inadvertently touch it and the room would go into darkness. I would put the light back on as quickly as I could to continue writing, but those few seconds of

72

darkness would distract me. Needless to say, it was very annoying. As my writing and the night went on, so did the aggravation of the lamp going out. I got so mad that I threw my pen down, put out the light and went to bed before I did something drastic.

I know you're thinking that maybe I'm over-reacting concerning the lamp, but remember where I am. In prison it's usually the small things that "set you off." You let the big disappointments build up, such as being turned down again for parole; not getting a job you really wanted; or having your wife or girlfriend leave you. Then out of the clear blue you find your hands around another inmate's throat, trying to squeeze the life out of him for not returning your TV guide, or for cutting out an article from the newspaper before you got a chance to read it.

Now that's the last thing I wanted to happen to me. I "liked" where I was, and in no way wanted to be transferred to a more strict institution for losing control. So when the lamp started to get to me (and it did), I would go out for a walk in the yard and fantasize. Well, actually I would daydream about the world, but some of my daydreams would turn into fantasies. For example, I would picture myself fishing at a quiet lake with a simple bamboo pole. Then, in the next scene, I would be out on the lake in a beautiful motorboat with a brand new fishing rod. Then I would say to myself, "When I get out, I'm going to buy a yacht with deep sea fishing rods, and head down to the Caribbean." Now this is when a daydream becomes a fantasy, because I don't have a penny to my name.

Even fantasies can run a muck, as in the times you are with your wife, and somehow you find yourself getting "dressed-up" for a bout of love making, instead of getting undressed. So there you are, looking like a half-dressed cowboy, or better yet like Tarzan, and you catch a glimpse of yourself in the mirror. You stop and stare and say, "What the hell am I doing?" A fantasy gone awry.

Well, back to the story of how a lamp can cause madness. The problem of the lamp going off and on continued night after night, week after week, and month after month. No matter how hard I tried to keep from touching it, somehow I would; and if I thought too much about the lamp, I wouldn't be able to concentrate on my writing. Then came "The Night."

Everything was going well—no, everything was going great. My roommate was sleeping without snoring (so I had peace and quiet); the lamp did not go out once, and the words were flowing out of my pen like diarrhea. For me not to accidentally touch the light and to have the ideas flowing from my head was a sign—this was my night to write. I was in the middle of a paragraph when a guard opened the door and said, "Lights out!"

"What?"

"It's 12:00—lights out!"

"What are you talking about? There's no such rule!"

"If you read the list of new rules on the bulletin board

that the superintendent wrote, you would know that's one of the new rules!"

So, desperately, I tried to reason with him about my writing, the trouble with the lamp, and to give me a break this once; but to no avail.

"Lights out!" he yelled. "Lights out, I want lights out!"

That did it. I lost control. Violent fantasies were running through my head. Everything got blurry. I knew I was yelling, but my voice sounded muffled in my head.

"You want lights out? You want lights out? I'll put your lights out!"

I picked up "the lamp" and smashed him in the center of his forehead. My light and his "lights" went out, and both fell to the floor; the lamp with a crash; the guard like a blanket held out at arms length and just dropped in a crumpled mess. The inmates opened their doors just in time to see the guards jump on me, handcuff me and drag me out—screaming and kicking. I was thrown into solitary, and just before I passed out I noticed there was no lamp on the table. I went to sleep whimpering, but with a smile on my face.

The next day I awoke and sat up on my bed. Well, I assumed it was the next day. I could have slept a couple of days; God knows I needed the rest. I looked around the cell. It had the basics: a bed, toilet and sink, and a table and chair. Then I noticed something on the wall, could it be? I went over to it slowly, yes, it was a light switch. I looked around, there was no lamp. I looked up at the ceiling and saw one single light bulb. I reached over and flicked the switch, the light came on. I flicked it again in the opposite direction and the light went off. This was good. I leaned on the wall and worked the switch. I watched the light go off and on—totally under my control. I rested my head against the wall, gently caressed the switch and smiled.

Days and nights went by. I found myself waiting for the sun to go down so I could switch on the light. And then, when it was time to sleep, I would switch it off. I was in full control of the light. But I must have played with it too often, because as I was flicking it off and on the bulb made a popping noise and went out. I sat on my bed in the darkness. "Now you did it," I said to myself. I started quietly cursing the light, electricity, lightning, the world, and myself in general, when the cell door opened. The light from the hallway came streaming in. The guard said, "I have some stuff for you."

"Stuff?" I asked, sheepishly.

"Yea, your mother and sister were here to visit you, but because you're in solitary confinement they couldn't see you. But they did leave you some things."

He went out in the hall and brought in a bag of food. "This is from your mother." Good old Mom, always thinking of my stomach. "And this is from your sister."

He placed a box on the floor and walked out. Just

before the cell door slid shut and the room went dark, I read on the side of the box, "This side up" and "Fragile." Slowly I went over to the box and read the card: *To my favorite brother, may this gift bring "sunshine" into your life. Love, Terry.*

What was she talking about, "Favorite brother?"— I'm her only brother! I opened the box and with the little bit of light that came in through the window in the door, I looked inside. There was a lamp—the same type of lamp I had in my other room. I pulled it out of the box and placed it on the table. Frantically, I felt around the base looking for a switch—there was none! I looked for a pull-chain— none. The lamp had no switch! It was the exact same kind of lamp that got me into this mess. I sat on the edge of my bed and once again the tension started—the headaches, the wringing of the hands, the erratic breathing, and then the fantasies; maybe I could take the cord and hang myself, if only there was something to tie it onto; maybe I could rip the cord out of the lamp, plug it into the wall and drop the other end into the toilet while I sit on it—if only it would reach; maybe I could unscrew the bulb and stick my finger in the socket, but I knew the shock would only knock me across the room and I'd still be alive—with a bad hairdo. Maybe I could...I sat there for hours listing all the maybes 'til I fell asleep, if you could call it that. Because all during the night I would dream about "the lamp," or at times, many lamps—all shapes and sizes—all without switches.

All the inmates could testify of my 'fear and hatred' of the lamp, for at least once a night they would hear the "cry"—a cry of desperation, of terror, a kind of mental torture.

They could only imagine what this poor soul was going through. Night after night, week after week, month after month it would echo off the walls of cell block #9- the cry of...

"No! No! Not the lamp!

Take it away! I don't want the laaammmp!"

POCKETS

There once was a little boy, who was a good little boy, well, good is such a relative term. You see, it depended on who was doing the judging. If it was his mother or father, he liked to hear them say, "He's such a good kid, he doesn't give us any trouble." But if it was his friends doing the judging, then he wanted to be thought of as bad—not real bad—just bad enough to have fun. You see, even though boys have fun playing ball, riding their bikes, climbing trees, etc; they also have fun stealing an apple or two from the neighbor's tree, going through trash barrels looking for "good stuff" and making a mess, throwing a rock through a window of an abandoned building which should have been torn down years ago, or pulling the hair of a girl.

Now, there's a tricky one—when it came to girls, boys wanted to be looked at as both good and bad. It's one of the first dilemmas we encounter growing up. Maybe it's because you know your girlfriend will grow up to be a mother, and you always want your mother to think of you as good; and yet she's your friend, which makes your bad (mischievous) side come out. So, because of that, you would find yourself walking a fine line between good and bad. At times it got confusing, but it wouldn't be the last confusing thing you'd do for women. It's too much of a deep subject to get into now. In fact, you could write a book on the relationships between men and women, and actually many people have. But now I want to change the subject, back to apples.

I had mentioned earlier about stealing apples. When I was about ten years old the gang and I had a favorite apple tree, along with a favorite pear tree, and a favorite cherry tree scattered throughout the neighborhood. Early in our escapades we learned not to mess with people's grapevines. The reason being, we found out that the families that had grapes, besides eating them as a snack, also made grape jelly and wine.

The children would play in the shade of the grapevine, look up and see "jars of jelly." Their father would lie in the shade while he listened to the baseball game on the radio, and look up and see all those grapes washed and in a bowl on the dining room table. And then there was the grandfather. He would sit in his wicker chair with the cushions broken in just right to fit his body, look up and see bottles of wine— "life's blood"—"bottles of happiness"—"glasses full of memories" (of friendships made and friendships lost).

There's another reason we left the grapes alone, Papa would always be in the yard sitting, or in the garden checking on the tomatoes, green beans, zucchini and countless other vegetables. And when we came too close to the fence where the grapevine grew down, he would stand up as straight as he could, wave his cane and in a stern but fatherly voice say something to us, mostly in Italian, which we understood as, "Move along boys, don't even think of it." So out of respect, we left that yard alone. It wasn't because we were afraid of the Mafia, or that one of his sons might come out and break our legs; or maybe it was. One thing Italian families didn't need for the backyard was a watchdog—they had Papa.

So, by now you're asking, "What about the apples?" Sorry, I have a habit of going off the track. And I should know better, because in school they were always teaching us not to mix apples and oranges, and here I am mixing apples with all kinds of fruits and vegetables.

So anyway, there was this apple tree with the biggest and juiciest apples that we used to "visit." One day the owner called us over and said that if we would stop sneaking into the yard and climbing his tree, he would give us the apples. It seems he was afraid of us damaging his fence or falling out of the tree. We agreed.

Weeks went by and he held-up his part of the bargain, and we lived up to ours. After a while we lost interest in the apples. They just didn't taste the same as when we took them. Those days were gone. If he saw us walking by he would hand us a bag of apples, we would thank him and move along. They never tasted the same again. I guess if I had to come up with a reason it would be that we didn't earn them—they were handouts. There was no reason to appreciate them; except for the fact that they were free, but that wasn't the reason we wanted them in the first place.

There was no excitement involved—no planning, no sneaking around the yard like Indians around and intruder's campsite. (To do the job right you needed three—a climber, a catcher and a lookout.) The thrill was gone. A part of childhood had been compromised. It was the start of the long road to adulthood, of being "responsible." If we only knew then what we were getting ourselves into, we would have said, "No way, Mr. Brown! And we challenge you to catch us!" and go running down the alley.

Well, a lot of life has passed since those "good old days." But what prompted me to write this story was my little boy's laundry, or more specifically his dirty dungarees. I was checking his pockets before I threw them into the washing machine and to my surprise they were empty! I stepped back a few feet and sat down—lucky for me there was a chair there. With my mouth wide open, my eyes glazed over and still clutching onto his pants, I swallowed and said out loud, "Empty?" My mind slipped back to days gone by (that's how I fell into the apple story).

When I was young, it seemed that I never had enough pockets, and his turn up empty? Where were the "things" of a boy's day? On any given day my mother would find countless things; a button (that didn't belong to anything I owned), a rock (a plain, everyday run-of-the-mill rock), a Popsicle stick (still sticky—used to get a closer look at ants), three pennies (just four more and I could buy a fudgesicle), a piece of rounded glass (a gem from a pirate's treasure), a dirty lifesaver (when it went in, it had the silver foil on it), a piece of string (not long enough to do anything with), a piece of paper (because of the color), a nail (there's always a need for something with a point, and I wasn't allowed to carry a jackknife—well not until I was 12 years old), a marble (for obvious reasons), and every once in a while, matches (and when that happened I would get a lecture and sent to my room for a day or two). The back pockets were reserved for baseball cards and a piece of linoleum

82

(saved for the pretty design or for "winging" it like a flying saucer). And this is just a sample of what could end up in a little boy's pockets.

Were empty pockets a sign of a troubled child? Will he turn to a life of crime as an adult because of it? Will the first signs of trouble show up when he's 11 or 12, with him getting along with girls, and not teasing them or pulling their hair? Am I failing as a parent? After all, isn't it a parent's job to teach a child everything he can? Yes! That must be it; it's all my fault. Sure, his pants have pockets, but no one ever told him what they're for!

I ran frantically into the backyard. "Oh, Jimmy! Oh, Jimmy! I have some 'stuff' for you!"

CHAPTER THREE

RELIGIOUS

This is the first poem I wrote in prison.

MOTHER MARY PRAY FOR ME,

TURN TO GOD TO SET ME FREE

MY HEART IS TRUE MY MIND IS CLEAR,

I LOVE YOU BOTH OH SO DEAR

PUT ME BACK IN MY WORLD,

SO I MAY TEACH EACH BOY AND GIRL

THE THINGS THAT MATTER, SUN AND MOON,

FEATHERS AND FUR, WAVES AND DUNES

AND WHO TO THANK FOR ALL THIS BEAUTY?

TO GOD ALMIGHTY WE OWE OUR DUTY.

This was when I was going to receive Holy Communion

after many years.

WELCOME HOME

As I prepare myself
To receive You once again,
The same pleasure returns
As in meeting an old friend.

I think back when -
My heart was cold and my soul was lost,
And how happy You must be
To have them both, at last.

I look forward to the precious time
When I get to stand before you,
And once again declare my love
And how much I adore You.

I stand before You with a grin
And my arms opened wide,
Waiting for you to come within -
Welcoming You to come inside.

A child opens his eyes wide
To take in all life's sights,
I open my heart for You to fill -with love and joy -
For all my days and nights.

My body is the Temple of Christ, So what I'm trying to
say in this poem, is—to put it simply—***Welcome home!***

9/24/90

The question was raised tonight at the Christian Fellowship Christmas party,

"Would you die for Christ?"

Some raised their hands, but I did not. I was very surprised and felt ashamed of myself because I know how much I love Jesus. I was thinking it over when right after the show of hands he asked,

"Who would live for Christ?"

My hand shot right up—I felt good. It's easy to say you'll die for Christ because chances are you will never have to. That's why I didn't raise my hand—it was too easy—it was expected.

In a sense, to live for Christ would be much harder, but I look forward to it. At times it will be a struggle but that's what life is about. And when you fall (fail), you get up and try even harder.

Remember, Jesus died in order for us to live—for ourselves, but through Him!

12/1/90

LESSONS FROM JESUS

"It is one thing to buy a house and love it;
It is another thing to build it and love it."

"It is one thing to take care of children and love them;
It is another thing to have a baby and love it."

"To learn about good living is one thing;
To live good is quite another thing."

"If you are good, do not come to me, go forth and do good.
For you can not come to me and get better, but you can get better by doing good."

Through your good works, Jesus will grow in you. People will see good in you and imitate you. The word of Jesus will spread by good works.

WOE TO THOSE WHO COMPLAIN

It's not my fault, if only it wasn't there.
If only you had no evil food (drugs),
I would not have eaten.

If only you had no knife,
and if only they had not made such a thing,
I would have not killed.

"But I say to you, there will always be such foods.
Some will heal and some will poison."
We must learn from Jesus, and our inner soul,
what is good and what is bad for us.

"For I say to you, if there were no bow and arrows,
or swords,
        or knives, then you would pick up a rock and kill."

There is no evil in God's earth, there is only evil in
man.
So on your knees pray to Jesus for forgiveness and
strength.

Why did Jesus come to earth?
Why did Jesus die for us?

If one falls, do you not have to bend over to pick him
up?

If weeds grow among your crop, do you not have to get on your knees to pull them?

We must humble ourselves in order to grow.
The greatest house starts with a solid foundation.

The tallest tree started as a lowly seed.

When a loved one dies, you must die also, in order to learn how to live.

To get closer to Jesus we must suffer the way of the cross with Him, and we must die on the cross with Him.
In that way we will be able to live with Him.

HEAVEN IS ALL AROUND US

GOD –

You are the tree of life. You give me joy and pleasure in what I see: babies & puppies, hugs & kisses, weddings & anniversaries, candles & balloons, birds & butterflies, trees & plants, mountains & valleys, oceans & lakes, sunrise & sunset, moon & stars, Mom & Dad and of course— rainbows.

My eyes are the windows to heaven, but also to hell. I could close my eyes to death and destruction, pain and suffering; but I would have to give up Heaven and You. I would then only have myself, which would dwindle to "nothingness" through loneliness.

So I thank you for my life, my health and my eyes—in order to see the pain and injustices—so I know what has to be corrected; in doing so I will increase the domain of Heaven.

Thank you for this honor,
Jim 7/8/91

It's not the fact that I exist that makes me believe in God, although it is a wondrous, mystical happening; it is the utter diversity of life-forms that boggles the mind, which can be offered as proof of the existence of God.

7/5/91

A PRAYER TO THE FORCE

POWERS THAT BE-
FROM THIS CONFUSION,
I MUST BE FREE.
I'VE TRIED IT ON MY OWN,
BUT I CAN'T DO IT ALONE.
I NEED YOU AND I LOVE YOU
I'M YOURS AND YOU ARE MINE.
TOGETHER WE CAN STOP TIME.
TO LOVE IS TO LIVE!
WITHOUT LOVE THERE IS NOTHING TO
GIVE.
WITH NOTHING TO GIVE
ALL YOU CAN DO IS TAKE,
BUT THAT'S NO GOOD—IT MAKES EVERY
THING FAKE.
YOU SHOWED ME THE WAY ONCE BEFORE,
BUT FOR SOME CRAZY REASON I SHUT THE
DOOR.
I DIDN'T MEAN TO IGNORE YOU
I THOUGHT I DIDN'T NEED YOU.
BUT I WAS WRONG,
I'M NOT THAT STRONG.
AND NOW I'M BACK
CAUSE I KNOW WHERE IT'S AT.
WE NEED EACH OTHER -
AS SISTER NEEDS BROTHER,
AS FATHER NEEDS MOTHER,
AS LOVER NEEDS LOVER.

THE TRIP

By a gift from God, by way of intelligence, man has invented and built a machine which can take us from point A to point B in relative comfort, with our favorite music and in the company of friends; and as an added bonus we have beautiful scenery to gaze upon. To enjoy this "ordinary" miracle you must appreciate the sights and sounds of the trip, drive carefully, and realize by the grace of God you are able to travel from one place to another and absorb everything along the way. When you arrive at your destination you will see that it's not the beginning of the fun. That started when you opened your eyes and your mind and said thanks to God for what is, and the opportunity to see more.

"GETTING THERE IS HALF THE FUN"

5/7/91

LOOK TO THE STARS

Return to yesteryear
To days gone by,
When blue skies filled the eye
And dreams filled the air.

When space was plentiful
And people and ideas roamed free -
Over mountains and rivers and the great prairie,
Back to the days of "America, the Beautiful."

When cowboys were men,
And even with all their courage -
Some prayed to heaven,
For Jesus to guide them.

No matter who you are
Or how far you've gone in life -
Cowboy, Indian Chief, or Housewife,
We all need that inner strength -
That's why we look to the stars.

The Angelus   Millet (1814-1875)
                                     The Louvre, Paris

BLESS US, LORD,
AND ALL THE GIFTS YOU GIVE US.

THE REWARD

He rises in the morning
Just before the sun,
And as sure as there are empty stomachs -
In both man and beast,
You can be sure that the job will be done.

From the kitchen table to the barn,
To the tractor, to the field.
The more the sweat drips
Off his chin and off his nose
And mixes with the dirt
The taller the plants seem to grow.

When the position of the sun
Tells him his work is done,
He back tracks to the table
To his wife, daughters and sons.

The joy of the day
Is to sit on the porch,
Look over the yard
And watch the children at play.
To smell the newly turned soil
Which is the farm's cologne,
And to sit back and realize -
This is where he belongs.

He finds himself gazing out over their heads -
The children, the cows and the dog just ahead,

To the land, in shades of browns and greens.
He now knows what it all means -
The closer to earth, the closer to GOD.

THE ROSE…AND SO LIFE IS

We grow,
We try our best to reason our purpose,
Fulfill our dreams,
Reach our full potential, but alas,
We are at the mercy of nature,
But we grow

We start out not knowing why,
Only that we must try.
Early in life, too soon it seems,
We learn about pain,
But we grow

Long and hard until we branch out
To absorb life's gifts -
Sunlight and knowledge, ah things are good,
And we grow

But then we learn of death,
Or a wrong path taken.
So we must "adjust" ourselves and continue
To grow

Into the most beautiful living thing we can be.
Oh what a glorious, wonderful and peaceful feeling
When we blossom!

Thank you Lord for the sun.
Thank you Lord for the chance,
To grow...

The rest of my life will be lived for the honor of Dad and the glory of God. I will fulfill Dad's expectations of me to the best of my ability by sharing the knowledge and insights he gave me by teaching (showing) the children what is important in life. Once Dad's "work" is completed through me, the teachings of Jesus will fall into place. Dad's "work" is an extension of Jesus.

For as -
The bush becomes the tree
And the river becomes the sea,
The son becomes the father
And the father is within me.

10/25/90
Jim

Things to leave behind so people will remember you:

children
a family business -the customer first, profits second
buildings—specially designed and well built
writings—from the heart, for the common person
paintings—pleasing to the eye, stress colors—not the
    scene
music—personal and simple

CHAPTER FOUR

FOR THE CHILDREN

"And as the wind blows.
So is the twig bent."

We should counter-act the ill wind that threatens our young, by giving them love, guidance and protection, so they may grow straight, tall and strong.

Straight—as in "going down the right path"
Tall—so they will see trouble coming
Strong—so they will be able to say "NO!" to temptation—and there will be temptation, there is no doubt about that.

So now is the time when they're young, to grab them and love them and point them in the right direction; for if this responsibility is put off, it may be too late to save the child in later years.

Each child is a brick in the foundation of our future and without a strong foundation the building will crumble. Love and teach the children and all will be well. If you ignore them and push them aside, all will be lost—the child, the family, and the country.

8/29/90

HALLOWEEN NIGHT

The heat is gone,
The coolness is here,
The days grow short,
Which just increases the fear.
Of the ghosts and the goblins
And the large green creatures with long black hair,
That reach out to grab you,
As you run through the door,
And yell, "Mom, I'm here!"
And you wish you didn't have to go out no more.

But this is that night,
That comes once a year,
In which we get all that candy,
As we ignore all our fears -
Of wolves, and owls and bats,
And black cats that just sit and stare -
Out through the window into the night,
Looking at shadows and leaves blowing by,
I'll say, "I don't care."
But inside I'll be saying, "I hope I don't die!"

You sit in your room,
Trying to get rid of the fright,
When your Mom comes to the door -
With a long, shiny knife,
You look to escape, but there's no way out -
All you know is, you must save your life.

You hope and you pray...
That you can save your skin,
You never thought you'd see such a terrible sight,
Then she says, "It's time to carve the pumpkin."

When she starts on the face,
She's so calm and relaxed,
But the more that she "slices and dices"
The more the knife becomes an ax!
She calls me over to see what she has done.
And to my horror, it stops me in my tracks.
Instead of a happy face -
She's made it look so gruesome,
Day is night, and white is black,
I wonder if "Mummy Dearest" is in fact a demon!

My time has come...
To go outside,
I dressed as a clown,
So my fear I could hide.
Out on the streets, there were monsters everywhere —
There was Wolfman and Frankenstein, Jekyll and Hyde.
Unearthly things walked the streets -
There were vampires and zombies and everything evil, When
asked if I was scared, "No," I said. But I lied,
And I'm pretty sure, between the shadows,
I even saw the Devil!

It's getting near midnight...
And with my bag almost full,
I know it's time for me to go home,
So on my friend's arm, I give a pull,

115

And the most grisly thing happens, it comes off in my hand! He
turned to me and smiled, so hideously and unnatural -
He had eyes like a cat's, skin green and hairy,
and teeth sharp as tacks.
Needless to say, it was quite a surprise,
To see your best friend, so horrible and fearful —
With "blood dripping" fingernails and a gleam in his eyes.

"Like a bat out of hell"
I ran down the street,
Away from the creature,
Away from the beast!

Why was I out? Didn't my mother know
That there are monsters and demons
out looking for a feast?
The wind was howling, the moon so bright,
This was the time of Halloween Night!

Out of the dark came a witch dressed in black,
The bag of candy I dropped—to hell with the treats!
She was flying behind me with her breath on my back!
Into my house I ran, and the front door was slammed!
I looked out the window. . . What's that over there?
A witch flying by, with an eerie cry -
"I'll get you next year, my sweet little dear!"

Hush! Did You Hear Something?

If you hear a coughing,
Coming from my coffin,
Please stop, and look inside.

Maybe even a knocking,
Followed by a rocking,
Please stop, and look inside.

Even though it may be shocking,
To reach over and unlock it,
Please, oh please, look inside.

Cause to everyone's surprise,
You just might find,
That I'm still very much alive!

And to prove to all,
I'll sit up straight,
I'll stand up tall,
And laugh at fate.

But something I must really do,
Before I actually do die,
Is to find the guy,
Whose job it was -
To bury me alive!

"The Challenge"
Or
"Things in the Dark"

Something had to be done. I was 10 years old and I was afraid of the dark. I realized most kids were, but I wanted it to be one less problem that I would have to deal with when I got older. Growing up, we always hear, "you're too old for that," or "only little boys do that," so it seemed that being afraid of the dark was something I was supposed to grow out of. "But when?" I asked myself. I was looking forward to going camping with my friends in a few years, was I still going to be afraid of the dark? (I heard the woods could be very creepy at night) Or what about when I'm walking home with my date after the school dance, was she going to protect me?

I figured this was a good enough time as any to do something about this problem, but what to do? How do I cure myself of this fear? Let me say now that this fear wasn't unfounded. This was a result of years of watching monster movies, and being scared by my older brother, who took such delight in working me into a frenzy by telling me stories at bedtime of monsters, that would rip the heart out of its victim and eat it, and for dessert would suck the eye balls out. Each time that happened I would run out of the room screaming and crying into the arms of my mother, who was watching TV and waiting for my Dad to come home from work.

118

My mother would put me back into bed and warn my brother not to scare me any more. "Gee, Ma! I can't even talk to my little brother?" he would say.

"No you can't, because you don't know how to talk nice! Now, both of you go to sleep." She would then go back to the living room, leaving the door open just enough for some light to come in.

After I calmed down and things were quiet—for about a minute—I would hear a gurgling noise, like a monster having trouble breathing, coming from you know who!

"Ma!" I would yell, and in she would come, flicking the light on and going straight over to Mike's bed. "One more time! If you scare him one more time, you're getting a beating!"

"He was making monster noises," I said.

"No Ma, I must have been snoring in my sleep," he said in his defense.

"That's a lie," I yelled. Pointing her finger at him, "One more time and you're in big trouble!"

"Okay Mom," Mike said. He turned to me, "Good night Jim, pleasant dreams," and rolled onto his side facing the wall, so we couldn't see him smiling. Mom left the room. That's when I knew there was a special place in hell for him, and all the big brothers all around the world who picked on us little guys.

Now back to the problem, and what to do about it. I decided to challenge myself, saying out loud, "I dare you to go down into the cellar and walk to the far end and back without turning on the lights!"

Without the lights on? I thought, *by myself!* It was too late, the challenge was made, I couldn't back out now. If I did, then I might never lick this problem—"Fear of the Dark."

The cellar I was going down into was an old cellar, not a clean, playroom type cellar. This one had boxes on top of boxes, old furniture scattered about, mirrors being store that, when the lights were on, would reflect your image and scare the crap out of you. This was a place where all kinds of spiders lived, and mice, and big, black beetles and other such bugs which scurried along the dirty, cement floor.

There was a large, coal furnace in the middle of the cellar and that was the main reason why my father and I would go down the cellar—to shovel coal into it to heat the house. Today houses use oil or natural gas in the furnace, but when I was ten we used coal.

The furnace was large and it was warm to stand beside it. When I walked up to it, I could see the red glow coming out of the adjustable openings in the door, shining on the boxes of "junk" all around it.   And when the door was opened, to shovel coal into it, the heat was intense! It was the closest thing to hell I could imagine. I've been down in the cellar hundred of times, but that was with my father and with the lights on. Now I was going down alone and in the dark.

There were parts of the cellar where we never went. There was nothing my father ever wanted or needed from that area—it was "no-man's land." It was at the end of the cellar—just where I had to walk to. Was this where "strange things" lived! Ghosts from beyond, monsters that always lived and never died, like zombies, or maybe creatures from another world that were sent here by intelligent life forms to see if they could survive on planet earth. But it turns out they're scared of us, so they hide in dark places and only come out at night—to eat! Or maybe there is a crazy, demented person that escaped and was hiding out. So you see, a kid does have reason to fear the dark. But I was getting older, and deep in my heart I knew there was nothing living in my cellar—I just had to prove it to myself.

I walked to the cellar door and unlocked it. I opened the door and started down the stairs without turning on the light. Halfway down it dawned on me; why do we keep the cellar door locked? I was having second thoughts, but I breathed in deep and continued down the stairs until I stood on the cement. It was pitch black except for a small amount of light at the far end of the cellar, which was coming in through the small cellar window and from the red glow from the furnace. With all the lights out, the fire that was peeking out of the cracks in the furnace door, looked like red eyes.

I couldn't see my hand in front of my face, so I walked very slowly towards the furnace—that was the halfway mark. When I stood beside it, I stopped to catch my breath. My heart was pounding! I enjoyed its heat because the rest of the cellar was cool and damp, maybe that's why I had chills up my back. I took a deep breath and continued on. My objective was to touch the back stone wall, and live to tell about it. Three quarters of the way into the darkness I thought I heard something. I stopped and listened. Could it be a mouse? Or just some loose dirt falling off the old stone wall? Or could it be "something else?" I wasn't going to turn back now, unless I heard a growl.

I had my hand out in front of my face feeling for the old, wood dresser that would let me know by touching it that I was about three feet from the back wall. When I made contact, I went to the left to walk around it to get to the wall. I always thought if anything lived down there that would be the place for it—behind the dresser in the corner. Slowly, I reached out to touch the wall. My hand went into cobwebs and spider webs before I touched the cold, damp, stone wall. I pulled it back, shook off the webs and spiders, and headed back the way I came; so far, so good. Now, if I could just make it out alive. Even if there were no monsters, I could die of a heart attack!

The way out seemed even scarier, because if anything was going to grab me, it would probably be from the back. Like a cold slimy hand with thin fingers and long sharp nails wrapping quickly around my neck, and tightly squeezing it while I swing helplessly in the air, trying to yell out for help; or having a small, wild creature run up and jump on my back, digging its claws into my lower back and wrapping its hairy arms around my neck, so it can gnaw at my head! Or could you imagine walking in a dark cellar and bumping into "someone" who was blocking your way out? Terror would strike! What to do? Which way to go? It gives me chills just thinking about it.

I focused on the light coming from under the door at the top of the stairs. Once I made it to the top, I knew I would be safe. I placed my foot on the first stair and grabbed onto the railing. I figured if something latched onto me now, I would at least have the railing to hold on to and pull myself up the stairs, away from "the thing" and a hideous death.

Rather than feeling safer since my journey was almost completed, I started to panic. *Under the stairs*, I thought. It could live under the stairs! This would mean, just about now it would be reaching out for my ankle. I ran up the stairs, slammed the door, and locked it.

"I did it! I did it!" I cried out loud. I took the challenge -looked fear in the face and beat it. I proved to myself that there is "nothing to fear, but fear itself." I was proud of my accomplishment, and felt a little bit older. It was my first step in becoming a man. And I learned there was no such thing as monsters and creatures—at least, not in my cellar.

The End
Jim
3/8/92

WHY ME?

Images of monsters and ghosts, Indians and cowboys, pirates and super-heroes and countless other costumes raced through his head.

"What can I be?" Jimmy asked himself, as he lay in bed. It was the night before Halloween and he still did not know what he would dress up as. His mother had warned him that he was running out of time, but had he listened? Nooooo! And now he was paying the price—anxiety had set in, and the more he thought about his problem the more confused he got.

He lay in bed with the covers pulled up to his neck and looked around his room trying to think of a Halloween costume, or at least to fall asleep—he had no luck with either one. His bedroom door was left opened so that just enough light came in. He remembered that when he was younger there was never enough light to go to sleep with, and how, over time, his mother managed to close the door more and more, until at its present position, it let in just enough light to cast shadows on the walls from all his toys and things. Shadows that at times looked like ghost heads peeking at you, or long, thin arms with scary fingers reaching out for a neck to squeeze. His room was a mess, which gave these shadowy shapes more opportunities to appear—here, there, and everywhere. Jimmy remembered that early that morning his mother had told him to clean up his room, but he said he was too busy—he would do it tomorrow. It was always "tomorrow."

Then, a strange noise got his attention. He opened his eyes wide and listened. (Why we do that nobody knows—opening your eyes wide does not improve your hearing, but Jimmy did it anyway.) He remained under the covers and let his eyes scan the room looking for what caused that noise. All the shadows seemed to be in their proper places—as if they could move on their own, or would! The noise came again. It was outside. It sounded like a thud and scraping type noise with a rustling of leaves. *Leaves,* Jimmy thought, *trees have leaves!* Then, for the first time, he realized it was pretty windy outside and that the tree was scrapping against the side of the house. Whew! That was a relief, not that he was "really" scared. He went back to thinking about his Halloween costume.

He thought of a vampire. "Yea!" he said out loud. "All I need is a black cape, some dark eye make-up and fake, sharp teeth dripping blood!" Just then there came an eerie, high-pitched scrapping sound from the same direction as before. Jimmy sat up and looked at the window. The noise happened again, but this time he saw the thin end of the tree branch being dragged across the glass by the force of the wind. He got out of bed and went towards the window. Suddenly, bolts of lightning flashed in the night sky, blinding him for a second, and a strong blast of wind and rain blew open the windows. They were the old fashioned kind, with hinges on each side and you pulled them in towards you to open them. The rain smacked him in the face and the wind pushed him backwards. He fell over one of his toys, which should have been picked up days ago, and landed in the corner, on top of more "stuff."

Jimmy looked up and from the light of a second bolt of lightning saw a shiny ax coming down towards his neck to hack his head off! He rolled to the side as quick as he could—it missed him. He wondered how or why an ax would be in his room. When he took a closer look, he saw that it was the blade of his ice skate on top of the hockey stick, which was leaning against the wall. *What fool put them away in such a manner,* he thought to himself. Jimmy wiped the rain of his face, or was that sweat? He ran to the window, forced the two sides shut and flipped the latch to lock them. He turned, leaned back and let out a sigh. Without any thunder, lightning filled the sky again, which flashed into the room and lit it up in such a way as to show off all the creepy-looking shadows, all at once! That was enough for Jimmy. In a second he was across the room, in bed and under the covers—shaking.

He felt that he had enough of this. He thought he could get through this on his own, but he was wrong. He let out a yell, "Mom! Oh Mom! Come here for a minute!" Five minutes passed—nothing—no Mom. He called out again and no one came. Where could she be?

Jimmy still had the covers over his head when he felt something heavy on the end of his bed. Could it be Mom sitting on the bed? He pulled the covers back just enough to see. It was a pumpkin! All carved out into a "Jack-o-Lantern."

It had a goofy look to it—large round eyes with a funny mouth that had square teeth, spaced unevenly. Did his mother come in and put it there? He sat up, "Mom?" Silence... "Mom, don't play tricks on me! Are you hiding at the end of my bed?"

There was no response. *Where did this pumpkin come from?* He wondered. Then it happened. The face on the pumpkin started to change. The eyes grew smaller and became devil-like. The teeth went from being square to sharp points, and the mouth turned into a sinister smile. Jimmy moved back against the pillow. "Mom!"

The new, scary face grew bigger—no the whole pumpkin was getting larger. Inch by inch it grew—in about a minute it doubled in size! And it kept growing. Jimmy had the covers up to his eyes, but not over his head. He couldn't stop watching this evil face getting bigger and bigger. He could have sworn that he heard it growl.

Bang!! It exploded! There was pumpkin guts and flesh all over the room; on the ceiling, on the walls, and on Jimmy's face! Back under the covers he went. "Mom! Mom! Mom!" Boy was he shaking. "Why is this happening to me, when there are so many bad, mean kids out there, who deserve it?" he whimpered. "Mom!" he yelled from under the covers.

More than ten minutes went by; she never came to see what was wrong. Where was she? He wondered if she was okay. Then something grabbed his foot and gave a pull. He pulled his foot away. It grabbed onto his other foot and gave a shake. Was this the monster that got his mother? He kicked free and let out a loud, terrifying yell, hoping to scare the monster away, if that was even possible.

"Hey! What's with you?" someone said. He didn't move.
"Mom, is that you?"

"Of course it's me."

Jimmy threw back the covers.

"Where have you been? Didn't you hear me calling you? Didn't you hear the explosion? And watch out for all the pumpkin guts!"

"What?" she said.

He looked around the room—there were no pumpkin guts or flesh.

"Sometimes you say the strangest things when you first wake-up. Now, wash up and get ready for school." His mother went downstairs to the kitchen. Jimmy sat in his bed. He could feel his heart still beating hard.

"Stupid, dumb dream," he said out loud as to convince himself that it all was just a dream. He got washed and dressed and went downstairs. Breakfast was eaten without any mention of the dream.

Jimmy kissed his mother good-bye, and just before he went out the door, he turned and said something to his mother that she didn't quite understand, but made perfect sense to him.

"Mom, I'm sure glad that Halloween comes only once a year. If it came any more often, I don't think I could hack it."

When he said the word "hack," chills went up and down his spine. He slammed the door and ran for the school bus, leaving his nightmare behind him.

THE END

October 31, 1991

GRANDMA' S SONG

GO TO SLEEP MY BABY
GO TO SLEEP MY DEAR,
JUST FLOAT OFF TO DREAM WORLD
KNOWING THAT I'M HERE.

GO TO SLEEP MY BABY
WHEN I TURN OUT THE LIGHT,
CAUSE PUPPY DOGS AND FUNNY CLOWNS
WILL DANCE WITH YOU TONIGHT.

GO TO SLEEP MY BABY
GO TO SLEEP MY DEAR,
JUST FLOAT OFF TO DREAM WORLD
KNOWING THAT I CARE.

GO TO SLEEP MY BABY
AND DON'T YOU BE AFRAID,
CAUSE DUCKY-DOS AND FLUFFY SHEEP
WILL SHOW YOU THE WAY.

RIDDLES FOR CHILDREN

What can you hold without your hands?
your breath

Why don't bananas snore?
They don't want to wake up the rest of the bunch

What goes up and never comes down?
your age

What goes around a yard but doesn't move?
a fence

Where do cars mostly get flat tires?
where there is a fork in the road

If you cross a bee and a doorbell what do you get?
a humdinger

What kind of pliers do you use in arithmetic?
multipliers

Why shouldn't you tell a secret to a pig?
because he is a squealer

What can run but can't walk?
water

What bird can lift the most?
a crane

Where do fish keep their money?
in river banks

Why do bees hum?
because they don't know the words

Who was the first to have a mobile home?
a turtle

What is the biggest building?
the library, it has the most stories

AUTOBIOGRAPHY

I grew up in a hardworking neighborhood called Dorchester, which is part of Boston. It was mostly Irish, Italian, and Polish Catholics. I went to a Catholic school and played in the Little League. I had a wonderful family and a playful, but mischievous childhood, which carried over into adulthood. So I was always getting into trouble from the age of 7 to 40. To this day I can't adequately explain why, except to say that I loved the excitement; the adrenaline rush of living life on the edge. Well, I paid for it and now I am trying to atone for it.

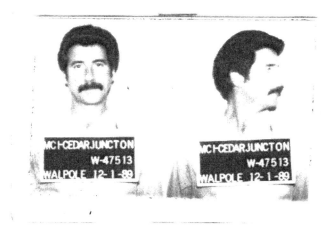

BEFORE

AFTER

(See Back Cover)

Made in the USA